The Mystery of
The Strange Bundle

The Tenth Adventure of
the Five Find-Outers and
Buster the Dog

Published by Granada Publishing Limited
in Dragon Books 1969
Reprinted 1970, 1971 (twice), 1972, 1973, 1974,
1975, 1976, 1977

ISBN 0 583 30124 X

First published in Great Britain by
Methuen & Co Ltd 1952
Copyright © Enid Blyton 1952

Granada Publishing Limited
Frogmore, St Albans, Herts AL2 2NF
and
3 Upper James Street, London W1R 4BP
1221 Avenue of the Americas, New York, NY10020, USA
117 York Street, Sydney, NSW 2000, Australia
100 Skyway Avenue, Toronto, Ontario, Canada M9W 3A6
Trio City, Coventry Street, Johannesburg 2001, South Africa
CML Centre, Queen & Wyndham, Auckland 1, New Zealand

Made and printed in Great Britain by
C. Nicholls & Company Ltd
The Philips Park Press, Manchester
Set in Intertype Times